The Quotation Bank for A-Level

The Duchess of Malfi

John Webster

Copyright © 2022 Esse Publishing Limited and Heidi Drake
The moral rights of the authors have been asserted.

First published in 2022 by:
The Quotation Bank
Esse Publishing Limited
10 9 8 7 6 5 4 3 2 1

All rights reserved. No part of this publication may be reproduced, resold, stored in a retrieval system or transmitted in any form, or by any means (electronic, photocopying, mechanical or otherwise) without the prior written permission of both the copyright owners and the publisher.

A CIP catalogue record for this book is available from the British Library.
ISBN 978-1-7396080-1-9

All enquiries to: contact@thequotationbank.co.uk
Every effort has been made to trace and contact all relevant copyright holders. However, if contacted the publisher will rectify any omission or error at the earliest opportunity.

Printed and bound by Target Print Limited, Broad Lane, Cottenham, Cambridge CB24 8SW.

www.thequotationbank.co.uk

Introduction

How The Quotation Bank can help you in your exams	4
How to use The Quotation Bank	5

Quotations

Act One	6
Act Two	12
Act Three	17
Act Four	22
Act Five	26
Critical and Contextual Quotations	31

Revision and Essay Planning

Performance History	41
How to revise effectively	42
Suggested revision activities	43
Glossary	44

Welcome to The Quotation Bank, the comprehensive guide to all the key quotations you need to succeed in your exams.

Whilst you may have read the play, watched a film adaptation, understood the plot and have a strong grasp of context, all questions in your A-Levels require you to write a focused essay, full of textual references and quotations (be they textual, critical or contextual), and most importantly, quotations that you then analyse.

I think we all agree it is **analysis** that is the tricky part – and that is why we are here to help!

The Quotation Bank takes 25 of the most important quotations from the text, interprets them, analyses them, highlights literary and dramatic techniques Webster has used, puts them in context, and suggests which quotations you might use in which essays. We have also included 10 contextual and critical quotations, analysed them, and linked them closely to the text, all for you to explore.

At the end of **The Quotation Bank** we have put together a performance history and great revision exercises to help you prepare for your exam. We have also included a detailed glossary to make sure you completely understand what certain literary terms actually mean!

How The Quotation Bank can help you in your exams.

The Quotation Bank is designed to make sure every point you make in an essay clearly fulfils the Assessment Objectives an examiner will be using when marking your work.

Every quotation comes with the following detailed material:

Interpretation: The interpretation of each quotation allows you to fulfil **AO1**, articulating an informed, personal response, and **AO5**, using different interpretations to inform your exploration of the text.

Techniques: Using associated concepts and terminology (in this case, the techniques used by Webster) is a key part of **AO1**, and can help you identify and analyse ways in which meanings are shaped (**AO2**).

Analysis: We have provided as much analysis (**AO2**) as possible, as well as exploring the significance and influence of contextual material (**AO3**) and different interpretations (**AO5**). It is a great idea to analyse the quotation in detail – you need to do more than just say what it means, but also try to explore a variety of different ways of interpreting it.

Use in essays on… Your answer needs to be focused to fulfil **AO1**. This section helps you choose relevant quotations and link them together for a stronger, more detailed essay.

How to use The Quotation Bank.

Many students spend time learning quotations by heart. This can be useful, but it is important to remember what you are meant to do with quotations once you get into the exam.

By using **The Quotation Bank**, not only will you have a huge number of textual, critical and contextual quotations to use in your essays, you will also have ideas on what to say about them, how to analyse them, how to link them together, and what questions to use them for.

These quotations can form the basis of your answer, making sure every point articulates an informed, personal response **(AO1)** and allows you to analyse ways in which meanings are shaped **(AO2)**.

The critical and contextual quotations allow you to easily and effectively explore the significance and influence of context **(AO3)**, and provide you with a variety of different readings to explore **(AO5).**

The textual quotations cover the whole text to allow you to show comprehensive whole text knowledge, and the critical and contextual quotations cover the full range of the text's publication history to help you explore the contexts in which the text was both written and received **(AO3)**.

Act One Scene One:
ANTONIO: "A prince's court/Is like a common fountain, whence should flow/Pure silver drops in general. But if't chance/Some cursed example poison't near the head/Death and diseases through the whole land spread."

Interpretation: Antonio expresses concern that corruption spreads through the community, leading to physical and metaphysical corruption. Political factions in the Jacobean court and the effects of patronage were key political issues of James I's reign.

Techniques: Simile; Epigram; Sentence Structure.

Analysis:
- Choice of "A prince's" in terms of gender separates the institution from the individual, foregrounding the difference between the public and private character of the ruler. It allows the point Antonio makes here to be generalised.
- "Cursed" hints at a supernatural element and/or the importance of evil, and the concept of damnation throughout the play as a whole.
- The positioning of the epigram "Death and diseases" foregrounds the effects of political corruption, foreshadowing the consequences of the events of Act One. Referencing "whole land" suggests such consequences will be inescapable.

Use in essays on… Death & Disease; Power & Patriarchy; Public Vs Private.

Act One Scene One:
BOSOLA: "Some fellows, they say, are possessed with the devil, but this great fellow were able to possess the greatest devil and make him worse."

Interpretation: Bosola highlights how evil and hypocritical the Cardinal is, establishing both the Cardinal and the Catholic Church as a source of immorality. This plays into contemporary fears around the power of the Catholic/High Anglican factions within the Court.

Techniques: Prose; Repetition; Hyperbole.

Analysis:
- Use of prose in Bosola's speech makes his place in the hierarchy clear; he is not using elevated language. This may also demonstrate the power of his feelings towards the cardinal – they can't be contained in structured verse.
- Repetition of "possess", as well as using the motif of the supernatural, also represents Bosola's position as a tool of the Cardinal.
- Suggesting that the Cardinal is "worse" than Satan ("possess the greatest devil and make him worse"), Bosola implies the Cardinal is behind the evil that will follow. We grow to trust Bosola's judgement.

Use in essays on… Supernatural; Morality; Religion & Faith; Power.

Act One Scene Two:
ANTONIO: "She stains the time past, lights the time to come.'

Interpretation: Antonio emphasises the Duchess' purity and her position as an example to everyone. She improves everything around her and is a figure of hope for the future. Throughout this long speech it is clear he puts her on a pedestal, representing purity as well as her own person.

Techniques: Chiasmus; Juxtaposition.

Analysis:
- The audience's introduction to the Duchess makes it clear she is more than just a woman. In her role as Duchess she is seen as a source of purity and goodness (compare her to the Gloriana presentation of Elizabeth I, for instance).
- "She stains the time past" demonstrates that she puts the "past" to shame, contrasted with the description of her brothers. "Stain" has connotations around sexual morality; is this perfection setting her up for a fall?
- The Duchess is associated with "light[s]" at this point of the play. Note how the play starts in light and ends in darkness; Act Five, after the Duchess' death, is particularly dark.

Use in essays on… Morality; Corruption; Appearance & Deception; Public Vs Private.

Act One Scene Two:
FERDINAND: "She's a young widow;/I would not have her marry again."

Interpretation: Ferdinand quickly makes clear what he wishes to avoid. He is her younger brother and has no real authority to make this so, resorting to underhand means to achieve his aim. If the Duchess remarries then he would lose any perceived control over her power and finances – as a widow the Duchess is relatively powerful.

Techniques: Language.

Analysis:
- The use of the first-person pronoun "I" foregrounds the fact Ferdinand believes this is about him. He is not acting in the Duchess' best interests.
- Emphasis on "young" serves both to belittle the Duchess in terms of authority and also highlight her vulnerability. She's a good "match" for someone (with contextual links here to Henry VIII's sister Mary, and Arbella Stuart) and it is natural to him there will be plotting around her future.
- Ferdinand often uses ambiguous language. The clarity of "she's a young widow" and the declarative statement "I would not have her marry again" is notable, perhaps implying some truth and logic to his statement.

Use in essays on… Power & Patriarchy; Morality; Corruption; Sexuality.

Act One Scene Two:
> **THE DUCHESS:** "Diamonds are of most value/They say, that have passed through most jewellers' hands."

Interpretation: The Duchess joins in the ambiguous word play in this discussion with her brothers. Her brothers attempt to persuade her not to marry again as it would, to some people, make her less pure; however, the Duchess' statement here makes it clear she does indeed intend to marry again.

Techniques: Epigram; Metaphor.

Analysis:
- In response to her brothers attempt to cheapen her, the Duchess compares herself to "diamonds", a jewel of great "value".
- It is of note the comparison is to a lifeless object of worth. The Duchess positions herself as a precious thing to be traded and "passed through" by man, rather than a human with a life and desires of her own.
- The choice of metaphor highlights the hypocrisy around the relative values ascribed to jewels and women.

Use in essays on… Power & Patriarchy; Morality; Corruption; Appearance & Deception; Public Vs Private.

Act One Scene Two:
THE DUCHESS: "All discord without this circumference/Is only to be pitied and not feared."

Interpretation: The Duchess demonstrates her naivete around the difference between her public and private persona. It is clear she has not realised the implications of what she has done for both the state and for her family. It is a private, personal moment that leads to public disharmony and destruction.

Techniques: Metonymy; Sentence Structure; Language.

Analysis:
- "This circumference" refers to both the ring and their small circle of confidantes who are privy to their secret. It should be a positive image but framed by "discord…pitied…feared", it is more ominous.
- Positioning "feared" at the end of a line draws the audience's focus to that word, rather than the "not" that precedes it. It makes the point less convincing, bringing an element of concern to a 'romantic' moment.
- Use of "only" belittles the response of her brothers as they have previously belittled her. All the siblings underestimate each other throughout the play.

Use in essays on… Power & Patriarchy; Morality; Appearance & Deception; Public Vs Private; Secrets & Lies.

Act Two Scene One:
BOSOLA: "I look no higher than I can reach."

Interpretation: Bosola's statement of motivation and self-improvement reassures the brothers he is no threat to the status quo. It is an ambiguous statement; in his role as a malcontent Bosola believes he can reach higher than the Cardinal and Ferdinand assume. His statement reassures them and as a result they underestimate him.

Techniques: Ambiguity; Repetition.

Analysis:
- The repetition of "I" in this statement focuses attention on individuality and individual responsibility. As a 'malcontent' Bosola is a 'new man' focused on ability rather than heredity for reward. His focus on individuality links him with the Duchess.
- By not giving a specific limit to his "reach", Bosola is able to state his real opinion without antagonising the brothers. They have already limited his "reach" in their minds due to his background; he extends his "reach" due to his ability. It may also serve to link Bosola with Lucifer (the great over-reacher.)

Use in essays on… Power & Patriarchy; Morality; Appearance & Deception; Public Vs Private.

Act Two Scene Two:
> ANTONIO: "She's exposed/Unto the worst of torture, pain and fear."

Interpretation: Antonio's response to the Duchess going into labour highlights the secrecy around this process at the time. This is not the Duchess' first child, but the language Antonio uses shows he was unprepared for the process; it also positions Antonio as a sincere and caring partner who seems to be genuinely good.

Techniques: Foreshadowing; Hyperbole; Ambiguity; Tri-colon.

Analysis:
- The tri-colon "torture, pain and fear" is hyperbolic at this point. It positions Antonio as a concerned father and husband at this risky time for the Duchess.
- "Exposed" is an interesting word choice – as well as demonstrating that the Duchess is in physical pain, it highlights the risk of her secret getting out and becoming "exposed" due to the noise.
- Whilst the statement here is hyperbolic, it also foreshadows what will happen to the Duchess in coming acts. Her labour is a cause of "torture, pain and fear" but not in the way that Antonio means here.

Use in essays on… Sexuality; Appearance & Deception; Public Vs Private; Secrets & Lies; Gender.

Act Two Scene Four:
THE CARDINAL: "You fear/My constancy because you have approved/Those giddy and wild turnings in yourself."

Interpretation: The Cardinal identifies Julia's jealousy as arising from her own infidelity. It highlights his own hypocrisy to the audience and perhaps gives an insight into the motivation of the brothers in their treatment of their sister.

Techniques: Metaphor; Dramatic Irony.

Analysis:
- "You fear/My constancy" – there is dramatic irony here as the audience know that the Cardinal is not trustworthy. If he has ignored his vow to chastity as a member of the Roman Catholic clergy, what else will he ignore about his faith?
- The repetitive use of the pronoun "you" serves to force the blame onto Julia for how she feels. This attitude towards 'emotional' women is common throughout the play – consider the contrast with the response to Ferdinand's emotions.
- By referring to her behaviour as "giddy and wild turnings" the Cardinal belittles Julia's actions as frivolous and changeable; he does not trust her.

Use in essays on… Power & Patriarchy; Morality; Appearance & Deception; Public Vs Private; Secrets & Lies; Sexuality; Corruption.

Act Two Scene Five:
> **FERDINAND: "A sister damned/She's loose i'th'hilts-/Grown a notorious strumpet."**

Interpretation: Ferdinand dwells on his sister's sexuality and declares that she is damned for her sin. He loses control of his thought processes and seeks refuge in offensive language, calling her a prostitute.

Techniques: Sentence Structure; Language; Dramatic Irony.

Analysis:
- By describing the Duchess as "loose" Ferdinand demonstrates that his sister's perceived sexual immorality damns her. His judgement of her, whilst turning a blind eye to his brother, highlights hypocrisy around female sexuality.
- The line "She's loose i'th'hilts" is several 'beats' short, giving Ferdinand a dramatic pause. This disrupted metre demonstrates his emotional state and his inability to reason at this point. He is uncontrolled.
- Resorting to the colloquial "strumpet" to describe his sister emphasises Ferdinand's loss of control. He strays from elevated language into coarseness. His slurs are heightened since the audience know his sister is married.

Use in essays on… Power & Patriarchy; Morality; Public Vs Private; Secrets & Lies; Corruption; Religion & Faith.

Act Two Scene Five:
THE CARDINAL: "There is not in nature/A thing that makes men so deformed, so beastly,/As doth intemperate nature."

Interpretation: The Cardinal warns his brother of the danger of emotion. The brothers are clearly very different, with one being cool and calm and the other hot-headed. It is clear at this point, and as the play develops further, that the Cardinal puts a premium on being composed and in control.

Techniques: Repetition; Juxtaposition; Foreshadowing.

Analysis:
- The repetition of the intensifier "so" suggests the extremity of the response the Cardinal describes, highlighting the apparent hyperbole.
- Webster foreshadows Ferdinand's lycanthropy by using "deformed" and "beastly", emphasising how extreme emotion is considered unmanly and animalistic.
- The juxtaposition of two different uses of "nature" demonstrates how man's character can be separated out of nature. In a play centred on two brothers and a sister, this raises the issues and debate around nature vs nurture.

Use in essays on… Power & Patriarchy; Appearance & Deception; Public Vs Private; Madness; Corruption.

Act Three Scene One:
FERDINAND: "The witchcraft lies in her rank blood."

Interpretation: Ferdinand positions his sister as a source of the evil and corruption currently running through the state. There is a sense as well that he is blaming her for his own personal experiences, as well as that of Malfi itself.

Techniques: Metaphor.

Analysis:
- By associating his sister with "witchcraft" Ferdinand implies she is evil. This is a sexualised implication. By acting on her sexual desires as a woman, the Duchess has aligned with the forces of evil (much like, for instance, Eve seducing Adam). The motif of the supernatural surrounds the Duchess and Ferdinand, perhaps linking with them being twins.
- He describes her blood as "rank". This implies the idea of corruption and a sense of her being 'spoiled'. By linking it to her "blood" there is also a sense that she has spoiled the perfection they once shared as siblings. The bond previously between them has gone due to her actions.

Use in essays on… Power & Patriarchy; Morality; Gender; Religion & Faith; Sexuality; Madness; Corruption.

Act Three Scene Two:
THE DUCHESS: "Whether I am doomed to live or die,/I can do both like a prince."

Interpretation: The Duchess asserts her authority through an appeal to her position and rank. This asserts the view that there is something higher or more noble about the ruling class, who would have been expected to set an example in everything to their people (at least publicly). This extended to how they left the world, as well as their actions on it.

Techniques: Juxtaposition; Repetition.

Analysis:
- By saying "live or die" at this point the Duchess suggests the outcome is not as important as her behaviour. She is above such concerns and she has confidence in her goodness, which can be seen in contrast with Cariola's response.
- The repetition of the personal pronoun "I" demonstrates that she finally grasps the consequences of her actions; it serves to make the confrontation domestic rather than political. It is not about the state.
- The use of "like" in "like a prince" implies the Duchess is not as confident in her position here as she sometimes appears (such as asserting, "I am Duchess of Malfi still".) Webster highlights the vulnerability of women in power.

Use in essays on… Power & Patriarchy; Gender; Public Vs Private; Religion & Faith.

Act Three Scene Two:
FERDINAND: "Dost thou know what reputation is?"

Interpretation: Ferdinand tries to force his sister to realise the impact on the public image of herself, her role and the wider family. "Reputation" was more critical to women than men since perceived purity and goodness was more important than the reality.

Techniques: Rhetorical Question.

Analysis:
- Ferdinand assumes that his sister has forgotten or ignored the importance of her "reputation" in her role and uses this to attack her at this point.
- He highlights that the Duchess has forgotten both her public role and responsibilities to her people and family, seeing herself only as an individual rather than a member of various groups. This struggle suggests much in common with other Early Modern tragic heroes (e.g. Faustus and Hamlet).
- Ferdinand emphasises their closeness, using the pronoun "thou". As his sister is both older and more powerful politically, this could also be a show of superiority.

Use in essays on… Power & Patriarchy; Morality; Appearance & Deception; Public Vs Private; Secrets & Lies.

Act Three Scene Two:
BOSOLA: "A most unvalued jewel/You have in a wanton humour thrown away."

Interpretation: Bosola confronts The Duchess over her treatment of Antonio. He clearly interprets Antonio as the moral superior in this relationship. As a fellow courtier he identifies with him and is appalled at the treatment of a former favourite.

Techniques: Motif; Dramatic Irony; Metaphor.

Analysis:
- Bosola compares Antonio to a "jewel", a motif that is often used for the Duchess to demonstrate someone of moral worth, but that is treated as a possession by those around them. Does this make the audience confront the Duchess' deceptive behaviour?
- Use of "wanton" has connotations of sexual immorality. Bosola is still unaware of the whole truth and has slipped into the same judgements as others; clearly female sexuality is immoral and to be judged.
- The audience know that the Duchess has done no such thing as to have "thrown away" Antonio. However, it suggests that she may have made a mistake in her folly.

Use in essays on…Sexuality; Corruption; Morality; Secrets & Lies.

Act Three Scene Two:
CARIOLA: "I do not like/this jesting with religion, this feigned pilgrimage."

Interpretation: Cariola warns the Duchess about her plan. She is worried that using a pilgrimage as a cover for running away (and therefore lying about your faith) is tempting fate and might anger God. For her, it is a performance too far.

Techniques: Repetition; Foreshadowing.

Analysis:
- Cariola makes a clear, unequivocal statement, demonstrating her dislike of the plan based on her strong faith. Pilgrimage was an important part of Catholicism.
- "Jesting" implies that what they are planning is little more than a game and a joke to the Duchess and Antonio. It is a foolish plan and one she is desperate to distance herself from.
- By using "feigned", Cariola demonstrates it is a performative pilgrimage rather than a genuine one. This playing with faith doesn't sit well with Cariola, and sits within the frame of supernatural power within the text. By drawing attention to this, Webster foreshadows the looming disaster for the Duchess's family.

Use in essays on… Religion & Faith; Morality; Appearance & Deception; Public Vs Private; Secrets & Lies; Corruption.

Act Four Scene One:
FERDINAND: "You were too much i'th'light."

Interpretation: Ferdinand rebukes his sister for being too open and not keeping things private that should have been. She has been too open for a woman of her position.

Techniques: Metaphor; Foreshadowing; Motif.

Analysis:
- Again, the Duchess is associated with "light" in direct comparison to her brother Ferdinand. What Ferdinand believes to be a rebuke instead has positive associations with "light". It echoes all the other times this image is used in the play, associating the Duchess with goodness.
- This line foreshadows the coming darkness within the play. The use of "too" suggests there is something wrong in what the Duchess has done, something uncontrollable. This is an issue for Ferdinand, who wishes to control his sister and implies the darkness coming.
- The Duchess' "light" shines on the behaviour of her brothers, making their wrongs appear greater in contrast. This tortures Ferdinand, so he has to act.

Use in essays on… Religion & Faith; Morality; Appearance & Deception; Public Vs Private; Secrets & Lies; Corruption.

Act Four Scene One:
FERDINAND: "That body of hers/While that my blood ran pure in't, was more worth/Than that which thou wouldst comfort."

Interpretation: In his argument with Bosola, Ferdinand makes clear he puts more worth on the Duchess' physical being than on his own redemption, as long as it meets his definition of purity.

Techniques: Metaphor; Motif; Pronouns.

Analysis:
- Blood purity has been important to Ferdinand throughout the play. Here it reaches its height as he implies that her body is worth more than his soul. The purity of his line must be protected (and avenged) at all costs.
- Whilst he at first appears to give the Duchess some value by calling the blood "my blood", it is clear he perceives them to be bound together and the Duchess as his possession. The division of aspects also implies he sees himself as the superior element in the relationship.
- His focus on the physical "body" at the expense of the metaphysical here demonstrates Ferdinand to be a fallen man, close to damnation.

Use in essays on... Religion & Faith; Morality; Sexuality; Corruption.

Act Four Scene Two:
THE DUCHESS: "I am Duchess of Malfi still."

Interpretation: Confronted with her death, the Duchess seeks refuge in her rank, enabling her to face what is to come with the dignity expected from her role.

Techniques: Motif; Adverb; Language.

Analysis:
- Throughout the play the Duchess as a person has been confused with her role. She is never given a name of her own. She herself struggles with the difference between being a public and private person. At this crisis point, she finally embodies the public role of Duchess and uses it as armour.
- The use of the adverb "still" at this point reminds the audience that she has misjudged her role throughout. From her perspective nothing has changed, whilst to the audience it is clear she is now embodying a more 'statesmanlike' role – particularly when compared to Act One Scene Two.
- Her simplistic language at this point demonstrates her need to be understood and not shrouding her points in elevated language. She does not defend herself at length.

Use in essays on…Public Vs Private; Power & Patriarchy; Death & Disease.

Act Four Scene Two:
> **FERDINAND:** "I bade thee, when I was distracted of my wits,/ Go kill my dearest friend, and thou hast done't."

Interpretation: Faced with the reality of what he has done, Ferdinand immediately tries to abdicate responsibility, implying that his orders should not have been followed. This has echoes of Henry II and Thomas a Becket, as well as Henry VIII's treatment of various advisors.

Techniques: Juxtaposition; Sentence Structure; Pronouns.

Analysis:
- Ferdinand's statement in parenthesis serves both to minimise the impact of his mental state by describing it as merely "distracted", and to absolve him of responsibility for his sister's death.
- The juxtaposition of "kill" and "dearest friend" is interesting. Ferdinand appears to suggest Bosola should have known not to follow the instruction for this reason. It also serves to support Bosola's position in not trusting Ferdinand.
- Ferdinand's use of "thee" and "thou" confirm his perceived superiority to Bosola and the contempt in which he holds him; he blames him for the death.

Use in essays on… Morality; Corruption; Power & Patriarchy.

Act Five Scene One:
ANTONIO: "For better fall once, than be for ever falling."

Interpretation: Rather than spending his life running from confrontation and avoiding his brothers-in-law, Antonio informs Delio that he is going to act now so that, one way or another, it will be over. This places him firmly in the Revenge Tragedy tradition, unlike Hamlet, who spends a long time considering his actions.

Techniques: Repetition; Foreshadowing; Language.

Analysis:
- The switch from the one off "fall" to the continuous "falling" suggests that Antonio fears that if he does not act, the punishment and fear due to his current situation will be ongoing and endless. He wants to bring things to an end.
- The association of "fall" with the 'Fall' of Satan and mankind is ominous in that it implies damnation looms over the final act. Antonio suggests he has very little left to lose.
- The repetition of "fall" pushes our focus on to this. There is a sense that Antonio will be in a lower position and will have to compromise his morality.

Use in essays on… Religion & Faith; Morality; Death & Disease.

Act Five Scene Two:
> DOCTOR: "A wolf's skin was hairy on the outside/His on the inside."

Interpretation: The Doctor reports Ferdinand's account of his lycanthropy. He has become a hunter, driven by his basest needs – an animal. The description makes clear that the torture he experiences is internal rather than external. His lycanthropy is a manifestation of the guilt he feels towards his sister and for his animalistic desires.

Techniques: Juxtaposition; Metaphor.

Analysis:
- Ferdinand's lycanthropy is a highly dramatic visual representation of his guilt. It demonstrates he has lost control of his animalistic desires and has become uncivilised and dehumanised. Control has been important to him throughout the play; without it he is lost.
- Juxtaposition between the "outside" and "inside" 'wolfiness' implies we have no way of knowing the internal struggle, nor the risk, a man may demonstrate.
- The use of a wolf has connotations of unbridled sexuality, hinting at darker reasons for Ferdinand's guilt.

Use in essays on… Appearance & Deception; Death & Disease; Secrets & Lies; Corruption; Sexuality; Madness.

Act Five Scene Two:

JULIA: "It lies not in me to conceal it."

Interpretation: The Cardinal takes this as a statement of morality on Julia's behalf and treats it as such. It is, however, Julia telling the literal truth whilst protecting Bosola. She cannot conceal the truth as it is already shared with a third person.

Techniques: Language.

Analysis:
- Julia's apparently clear language actually serves to cover Bosola's spying in the moment. Julia is telling an incomplete truth as she does not give the reason she can't hide the Cardinal's revelation.
- By assuming it is Julia's morality that causes this, the Cardinal forces us to compare the morality of the female characters with the male. Secrets held by women do not last long in this play and are easily discovered.
- Women's language is often simpler and not designed to distract and obfuscate. This may be why the Cardinal underestimates Julia and is so confident that, in killing her, his secret is safe.

Use in essays on… Morality; Appearance & Deception; Public Vs Private; Secrets & Lies; Corruption; Power & Patriarchy.

Act Five Scene Four:
THE CARDINAL: "The devil takes away my heart/For having any confidence in prayer."

Interpretation: By finding himself unable to pray, the Cardinal is demonstrating how far he has sunk from his religious calling – this moment has echoes of Macbeth's failure to say 'amen' when going to kill Duncan. Only the damned would be unable to pray, and it is guilt that makes him unable to ask for God's help.

Techniques: Metaphor.

Analysis:
- By placing responsibility on "the devil" for his current situation, the Cardinal, like his brother before him, is distancing himself from the responsibility for his sin and therefore his guilt.
- The use of "confidence" is noteworthy in that it demonstrates the Cardinal has apparently lost his faith in God's ability to save him. Too late to change course, he has realised that his sinfulness has consequences.
- To a contemporary audience he represents the corrupt Catholic church brought low through its own failings.

Use in essays on… Religion & Faith; Morality; Secrets & Lies; Corruption.

Act Five Scene Five:
BOSOLA: "Thou, which stood'st like a huge pyramid/Begun upon a large and ample base,/Shalt end in a little point."

Interpretation: Bosola explores how, despite their attempts to be powerful, Ferdinand and the Cardinal will be forgotten. For all the advantages they possessed ("ample base"), they've thrown it all away in pursuit of more and have ended in a pointless nothingness. It is the sort of nihilistic comment that malcontents often voice.

Techniques: Simile; Metaphor.

Analysis:
- The simile of the "pyramid" highlights the absolutist power and fame that the brothers sought. By using a simile, Bosola makes it seem like it was always a façade and was never reality.
- By using a metaphor for the second half of the image ("little point") the reality of the pointlessness of all that has occurred is made clear.
- Their attempts to control the Duchess have failed and instead of securing their future, they destroyed it and will be forgotten.

Use in essays on… Morality; Appearance & Deception; Public Vs Private; Secrets & Lies; Corruption; Power & Patriarchy.

Lewis Theobald (1735) describes the play as,
  "a strong and impetuous genius but withal a most wild and undigested one."

Interpretation: Theobald sees Webster's work as that of a flawed genius. This was the common view of Webster's work from the re-opening of the theatres and into the 18th Century. Theobald, speaking about the play in production, feels it does not fit with expectations about what plays should be.

Analysis:
- The Duchess' death in Act Four is seen by some as too soon for the protagonist to die in a tragedy, and that without her the play is left rudderless. This misses part of Webster's point; the state disintegrates into chaos once she is murdered. This criticism also demonstrates how we view texts through our own lenses, with the 18th Century revisiting lots of early modern texts.
- The nihilism of certain elements of the play, for example Bosola's plot line, is seen as uncontrolled ("most wild") and an unnecessary ("impetuous") cruelty in its bleakness, rather than a necessary element of the plot that speaks deeply of human motivations.

Use in essays on… Power & Patriarchy; Corruption; Death & Disease.

'H.M' (1818) suggests that, after the Duchess' death, "our sympathies suddenly awakened, are allowed to subside."

Interpretation: The reviewer referred to as H.M. is in no doubt that much of the characterisation in the play is flawed, and that the audience do not get full catharsis from the experience of the play. This assumes Webster's intentions were focused solely on character, rather than critiquing the societal situations they find themselves in, and the way they act in them. This is the tragedy of a state, not an individual.

Analysis:
- When she claims "I am Duchess of Malfi still", the Duchess points out the flaw in H.M's reasoning. She is killed not only as a person, but as a head of state. It is perhaps society itself we are meant to have our "sympathies suddenly awakened" to within this play; arguably that sympathy does not subside.
- That said, it cannot be denied that this is a highly unusual play in having the main sympathetic character killed off in Act Four, with the remaining characters either unsympathetic or underdeveloped to contemporary tastes; is it fair to suggest the audience's "sympathies…subside" after the Duchess' death?

Use in essays on… Public Vs Private; Power & Patriarchy; Corruption.

> **Reviewing Richard Henry Horne's adaptation, *The Musical World* (1850) argues, "the revolting nature of the story, and the anti-climax of the fifth act in which the several villains kill one another, are beyond the reach of the reformer's skill."**

Interpretation: Critics continued to find issue with the play into the Victorian Era. Clear resolutions and character-focused plays were popular and this, coupled with the violence in the play, led to it being labelled "revolting". This critic's review gives us all the reasons why it was unpopular in the Victorian era, yet perhaps failing to realise the importance of those elements.

Analysis:
- The "revolting" elements (dismembered hands, fake corpses, on stage murders) are intentionally so. They are deliberately graphic representations of a corrupt and corrupting state; it is meant to revolt and disgust to add to the sympathy the audience feel for characters at various points, demonstrating Webster's "skill".
- The fifth act is not an "anti-climax" but rather a cleansing of the corruption of the state. The death of the 'new men' Antonio and Bosola leaves it as an untidy one ideologically; the audience must reach their own conclusions on the best way forward.

Use in essays on… Power & Patriarchy; Corruption; Death & Disease; Gender.

Rupert Brooke (1916) asserts,
   "Characters in a play gain realism if they act unexplainedly on instinct, like people in real life, and not on rational and publicly-stated grounds."

Interpretation: Both during and after the First World War, Webster saw a rise in popularity. Many critics, like Brooke, saw in his irrational and violent characters something more realistic, in the face of Total War, than popular contemporary works by Ibsen focusing on middle class issues. The emotional responses and immediate actions of the Duchess' world appear more human when looked at in this way.

Analysis:
- The Duchess' "unexplainedly" impulsive seduction of Antonio, instead of making her seem foolish and an unconvincing characterisation of a ruler, depict her as flawed and human – a person "in real life" – therefore making her more, not less sympathetic to an audience.
- Antonio's decisions, both to fly the court alone and return for reconciliation and then vengeance, also benefit from consideration in this light. As a good person this makes sense as his instinctive response; he acts "in real life, and not on rational and publicly-stated grounds".

Use in essays on… Power & Patriarchy; Corruption; Appearance & Reality.

M.C. Bradbrook (1935) believes that,
"In law the Duchess was innocent; by social standards she was at first reckless and intemperate; by ethical and religious standards she was an instinctive creature awakened by suffering to maturity."

Interpretation: Bradbrook led a change in criticism of the play. The Duchess becomes an intriguing figure in her own right. Her moral responsibility for what occurs depends on the individual audience member's position; this is not a play that deals in moral absolutes.

Analysis:
- The Duchess is not 'wrong' in anything that she does in legal terms, even at the time the play is set. Morality, however, is not the same as legality, as the differing responses of various characters make clear to us. From some perspectives, the torture she goes through in Act Four is required to save her soul and restore "religious standards".
- This approach foregrounds historical context whilst allowing for its complexity. There was no one response to the Duchess. It hints at the concern around female sexuality we see expressed by Ferdinand and the Cardinal, particularly in her as an "instinctive creature".

Use in essays on… Power & Patriarchy; Public Vs Private; Religion & Faith; Morality.

Lee Bliss (1983) argues The Duchess,
> "seeks private happiness at the expense of public stability."

Interpretation: Lee Bliss' clear statement on the flaw at the centre of the Duchess' downfall is astute in its approach to the political nature of the play. The conflict between public and private necessities becomes a central concern of early modern theatre and links the play to works such as *Hamlet*. The Duchess' error, according to Bliss, is to consider herself an independent, private person, rather than an institution.

Analysis:
- By seeking "private happiness" the Duchess creates a stream of secrets that becomes uncontrollable. Here she can be seen as a direct contrast to Elizabeth I, who was hugely conscious of this duality of existence and the loss of private self (although hints at the rumours surrounding possible heirs of Elizabeth).
- The destructive nature of the ruler seeking "private happiness" in the form of secrecy is clear throughout the play, leading to the complete failure of the state and "public stability". Could this be seen as a veiled warning to James I to avoid making the same mistake?

Use in essays on… Public Vs Private; Secrets Vs Lies; Appearance Vs Reality.

Lisa Jardine (1983), when discussing the Duchess, suggests,
  "she is metamorphosed from ideal mirror of virtue […] into lascivious whore."

Interpretation: Unlike other critics (e.g. Luckyj), Jardine is more critical of the Duchess' choices within the play. Her behaviour is equated with that of Gertrude and it is suggested we should judge her in a similar way. Her fall becomes one purely of sexuality here ("lascivious whore"), rather than more focused on the political significance of that sexuality.

Analysis:
- Antonio and Delio become important here as they highlight the Duchess' "virtue" and set her up as the perfect woman. This simplistic interpretation of the role of women places them in the virgin/whore dichotomy. By positioning her as Madonna-like at this stage, the Duchess is being set up to fall.
- If the Duchess is to perceived as only a "lascivious whore" from the point of her remarriage, the focus has to be on moments such as the eating of the "apricocks" rather than on her dignity in imprisonment, torture and death. Is she more complex than the dichotomy of "virtue" and "whore"?

Use in essays on… Power & Patriarchy; Corruption; Sexuality; Morality.

Frank Whigham (1985) argues Ferdinand is a,
  "threatened aristocrat, frightened by the contamination of his ascriptive social rank and obsessively preoccupied with its defence."

Interpretation: Whigham's class-based critique of the play was one of the first to explore motivations for Ferdinand's apparent incestuous desire for his sister. He sees Ferdinand as someone who fears the "social" change and mixing that is occurring. In its exploration of class consciousness, this is a Marxist reading.

Analysis:
- Ferdinand is so desperate to protect the purity of his class that his desire becomes limited to his own family (and indeed twin). In his fear of the new world he is as alienated from society as a result of class as Bosola is (look at how Ferdinand speaks to courtiers).
- By marrying Antonio, the Duchess pollutes ("contamination") Ferdinand's own bloodline. This threatens his own self-image as a 'pure' member of the ruling "aristocrat" class; this is what causes his mental breakdown as his self-ideation disintegrates.

Use in essays on… Power & Patriarchy; Corruption; Madness.

Christina Luckyj (1989) states Julia's,
"startlingly casual murder casts new light retrospectively on the psychotic forces behind the murder of the Duchess, showing them to be merely exaggerations of forces that regularly destroy women in the real world."

Interpretation: Despite being a feminist reading of the play, Luckyj shifts the focus on to the men. It is their uncontrolled and distorted ideals of masculinity and reputation that results in the deaths of all the women in the play. The play uses hyper-reality to critique society as much as politics, and gives voice to the often voiceless victims.

Analysis:
- The Duchess is not a victim of her own actions, but is a victim of her brothers' response to those actions ("forces"). Their perceived ownership of her is what "destroy[s]" them all, not her relationship with Antonio.
- The "startlingly casual" way the Cardinal goes about killing Julia serves to present femicide as normal and inevitable from his perspective, rather than a "psychotic" act. She is less than him due to her gender and can be treated as such; she is just cast aside.

Use in essays on… Power & Patriarchy; Sexuality; Morality.

Michael Billington (2014) declares the Duchess is,
"the image of endurance and fortitude."

Interpretation: Michael Billington's review of Shakespeare's Globe production in 2014 shows another development in the perception of the Duchess. He elevates her to stoic saint in the face of everything she experiences instead of a flawed ruler, patriarchal victim, or "whore". She is statesmanlike as the state disintegrates around her, in contrast with Jardine's interpretation.

Analysis:
- The Duchess in Act Four contrasts with Cariola's desperation and Julia's black comedy in the face of death. She is elevated above the other women in the play, and presented as an ideal comparatively (link back to descriptions of her in Act One, for example). She dies, but does not fall, in this reading.
- If the Duchess is the ideal woman (if not necessarily the ideal ruler) then does this mean that "endurance and fortitude" are the ideal *for* women? Or do these qualities lead to her nobility which is the real ideal? There is some ambiguity here.

Use in essays on… Power & Patriarchy; Gender; Sexuality; Religion and Faith.

Performance History

The Duchess of Malfi was often seen as too grotesque or unrealistic, and was rarely performed without adaptation in the 18th and 19th Century, yet the play is based on true events. In the late 15th Century the Duchess of Amalfi became a widow at 19 years old, married beneath her and had a child, all before vanishing secretly at her brothers' behest. To some extent, those who challenge the realism of the play's premise are blind to the social behaviours Webster sought to expose.

To many, the Duchess is a political figure, part of the institution she represents; for others she is an autonomous, independent individual. In exploring Webster's motivations, one can examine his source material, William Painter's *Palace of Pleasure* (1567); differences between the two highlight Webster's thematic concerns. Both begin with a Duchess of moral goodness, but Painter's sympathies dissipate, his anger falling on the Duchess' sexual desires and Antonio's breaking of social norms. Webster subverts this reading; his play ends with Delio restoring in the Duchess' son his "mother's right"; the personal supplants the political, and the Duchess' and Antonio's son is set to reign.

Scenes of lycanthropy and mutilation were often considered crude and were omitted, particularly in the Victorian era; whilst similar contemporary tragedies had graphic representations of a tragic character (think *Macbeth*, *Hamlet*, *Othello* or *King Lear* for instance,) *The Duchess of Malfi*'s constant graphic scenes perhaps highlight the tragic nature of the state as a whole. After WWII, the play was restored to what we often see today. In the Theatre Royal production of 1945, the depraved depths of human cruelty present in the play were no longer unrealistic or alien; humans torturing, mutilating and abusing the weak for their own insane purposes made Webster's message of the dangers of a corrupt state more pertinent and relevant than ever. The dichotomy between grotesque melodrama and insightful social criticism were brought together; rather than be mutually exclusive, Webster makes clear the political, public sphere is just as debauched and corrupt as the private, personal individuals within it.

How to revise effectively.

One mistake people often make is to try to revise EVERYTHING!

This is clearly not possible.

Instead, once you understand the text in detail, a good idea is to pick five or six major themes, and four or five major characters, and revise these in great detail. The same is true when exploring key scenes – you are unlikely to be able to closely analyse every single line, so focus on the *skills* of analysis and interpretation and then be ready for any question, rather than covering the whole text and trying to pre-prepare everything.

If, for example, you revised The Cardinal and Power & Patriarchy, you will also have covered a huge amount of material to use in questions about Morality, Corruption and The Duchess.

It is also sensible to avoid revising quotations in isolation; instead, bring together two or three textual quotations as well as a critical and contextual quotation so that any argument you make is supported and explored in detail.

Finally, make sure material is pertinent to the questions you will be set. By revising the skills of interpretation and analysis you will be able to answer the actual question set in the exam, rather than the one you wanted to come up.

Suggested Revision Activities

A great cover and repeat exercise – Cover the whole page, apart from the quotation at the top. Can you now fill in the four sections without looking – Interpretations, Techniques, Analysis, Use in essays on…?

This also works really well as **a revision activity with a friend** – cover the whole page, apart from the quotation at the top. If you read out the quotation, can they tell you the four sections without looking – Interpretations, Techniques, Analysis, Use in essays on…?

For both activities, could you extend the analysis and interpretation further, or provide an alternative interpretation? Also, can you find another quotation that extends or counters the point you have just made?

Your very own Quotation Bank! Using the same headings and format as The Quotation Bank, find 10 more quotations from throughout the text (select them from many different sections of the text to help develop whole text knowledge) and create your own revision cards.

Essay writing – They aren't always fun, but writing essays is great revision. Devise a practice question and try taking three quotations and writing out a perfect paragraph, making sure you add connectives, technical vocabulary and sophisticated language.

Glossary

Dramatic Irony – When the audience knows something the characters don't: when the Cardinal tells Julia "You fear/My constancy", there is dramatic irony here as the audience know that the Cardinal is not trustworthy.

Foreshadowing – When the writer alludes to or makes reference to something that is yet to come in the text: the positioning of the epigram "Death and diseases" foregrounds the effects of political corruption, foreshadowing the consequences of the events of Act One.

Hyperbole – An exaggerated statement that intensifies or adds emphasis: whilst the statement, "she's exposed/Unto the worst of torture, pain and fear" is hyperbolic, it also foreshadows what will happen to the Duchess in coming acts.

Juxtaposition – Two ideas, images or words placed next to each other to create a contrasting effect: juxtaposition between the "outside" and "inside" 'wolfiness' implies we have no way of knowing the internal struggle, nor the risk, a man may demonstrate.

Language – The vocabulary chosen to create effect.

Metaphor – A word or phrase used to describe something else so that the first idea takes on the associations of the second: by using a metaphor for the second half of the image ("little point") the reality of the pointlessness of all that has occurred is made clear.

Motif – A significant idea, element or symbol repeated throughout the text: Bosola compares Antonio to a "jewel", a motif that is often used for the Duchess to demonstrate someone of moral worth, but that is treated as a possession by those around them.

Prose – Normal spoken or written language, instead of verse: use of prose in Bosola's speech makes his place in the hierarchy clear; he is not using elevated language.

Repetition – When a word, phrase or idea is repeated to reinforce it: the repetition of the personal pronoun "I" demonstrates that the Duchess finally grasps the consequences of her actions.

Rhetorical Questions – A persuasive device where the person asking the question already knows the answer: Ferdinand assumes that his sister has forgotten or ignored the importance of her "reputation" in her role and uses this to attack her at this point with the question "Dost thou know what reputation is?"

Sentence Structure – The way the writer has ordered the words in a sentence to create a certain effect: the line "She's loose i'th'hilts" is several 'beats' short, giving Ferdinand a dramatic pause. This disrupted metre demonstrates his emotional state and his inability to reason at this point.

Simile – A comparison of one thing with something of a different kind, used to make a description more vivid: the simile of the "pyramid" highlights the absolutist power and fame that the brothers sought. By using a simile, Bosola makes it seem like it was always a façade and was never reality.

Tri-colon – A list of three words or phrases for effect: the tri-colon "torture, pain and fear" is hyperbolic at this point. It positions Antonio as a concerned father and husband at this risky time for the Duchess.

Acknowledgements:

L Theobald: *Preface* to *The Fatal Secret* 1735

'H.M': *Blackwood's Magazine* March 1818

The Musical World No 47 Vol XXV, Published by Nassau Steam Press 1850

R Brooke: *John Webster and the Elizabethan Drama,* Published by Sidgwick and Jackson 1916

M C Bradbrook: *Themes and Conventions of Elizabethan Tragedy,* Published by Cambridge University Press 1935

L Bliss: *The World's Perspective: John Webster and the Jacobean Drama*, Published by Rutgers University Press 1983

L Jardine: *Still Harping on Daughters: Women and Drama in the Age of Shakespeare,* Published by The Harvester Press 1983

F Whigham: *"Sexual and Social Mobility in The Duchess of Malfi." PMLA 100, no. 2*, Published by Cambridge University Press 1985

C Luckyj: *A Winter's Snake: Dramatic Form in the Tragedies of John Webster*, University of Georgia Press 1989

M Billington: *The Guardian* 16th January 2014